Dedication

To all the USUI Reiki trainers and practitioners of the world who are keeping the original Usui Reiki alive.

To my wonderful daughter Aashina Vyas for the motivation to pen this down. This book would not have been possible without her relentless support.

To all my family and friends who believe in me and the work I do. I'm so grateful to all of them.

7 CHAKRAS CHEAT SHEET.

Your 7 major Chakras are the gateways that connect you to the Universal Energy that's all around you. When they are balanced, they absorb this energy and send it throughout your physical and spiritual bodies to keep them healthy. When they are unbalanced, you may develop problems in your health, relationships, and life.

UPPER CHAKRAS (Spiritual Plane)

7. Crown Chakra
Color: Violet
Element: Space/Spirit
Location: Above Head
Psychological Function: Spiritual Connection
Body Function: Upper Brain, Right Eye
Aura Layer: Ketheric Template
Balanced: Connection to the Universe, Clear Spiritual Path, Empathy Toward All Beings
Unbalanced: Confusion, Attachment to Material World, Chronic Exhaustion, Spinal Disease

6. Third Eye Chakra
Color: Indigo
Element: Light
Location: Forehead
Psychological Function: Intuition
Body Function: Lower Brain, Left Eye, Ears, Nose, Nervous System
Aura Layer: Celestial Body
Balanced: Intuition, Clear Thinking, Ease in Decision Making
Unbalanced: Overly Analytical, Distrusting, Anxious, Insomnia, Migraines, Vison Problems

5. Throat Chakra
Color: Blue
Element: Ether
Location: Throat/Neck
Psychological Function: Communication Center
Body Function: Lungs, Vocal Chords, Esophogous, Respiratory System
Aura Layer: Etheric Template Body
Balanced: Clearly Express Ideas, Speak Your Truth, Offer Sound Advice
Unbalanced: Lying, Gossip, Verbal Abuse, Thyroid Disorders, Chronic Neck/Shoulder Pain

MIDDLE CHAKRA (Bridge Between Planes)

4. Heart Chakra
Color: Green
Element: Air
Location: Center of Chest
Psychological Function: Love & Compassion
Body Function: Heart, Blood, Circulatory System, Vagus Nerve
Aura Layer: Astral Level
Balanced: Feelings of Love, Compassion, Caring; Sense of Openness to Life
Unbalanced: Antisocialism, Manipulative Behaviors, Heart Disease, Breathing Problems

LOWER CHAKRAS (Physical Plane)

3. Solar Plexus Chakra
Color: Yellow
Element: Fire
Location: Above Navel
Psychological Function: Willpower
Body Function: Stomach, Liver, Gallbladder, Nervous System
Aura Layer: Mental Body
Balanced: Motivation, Connection to Sense of Purpose, Personal Power
Unbalanced: Poor Self-Esteem, Obsession with Perfection, Judmental, Digestive Issues

2. Sacral Chakra
Color: Orange
Element: Water
Location: Lower Back
Psychological Function: Sexuality & Creativity
Body Function: Reproductive System
Aura Layer: Emotional Body
Balanced: Warm & Friendly Personality, Stable Emotions, Meaningful Relationships
Unbalanced: Rollercoaster of Emotions, Depression, Sexual Dysfunction, Reproductive Issues

1. Root Chakra
Color: Red
Element: Earth
Location: Bottom of Tailbone
Psychological Function: Safety & Stability
Body Function: Spinal Column, Kidneys
Aura Layer: Etheric Layer
Balanced: Confidence, Control, Will to Live
Unbalanced: Irrational Fears, Unhealthy Cravings, Constipation, Obesity

FIND
YOUR
PATH

RE-ENERGISE WITH REIKI IN 21 DAYS

NANDA SHARAD

INDIA · SINGAPORE · MALAYSIA

Foreword

I fell in love with Reiki more than 2 decades ago, and it's an ongoing affair.

Reiki became my support system after I understood and experienced the power of Reiki. There have been multiple occasions where I have witnessed healings and instances which have been termed as miracles.

My journey with Reiki began in the year 2000 when a first-degree channel, Nita, healed me from a condition that had made not only my movements difficult but also my life miserable. When the doctors failed to decipher why the pain was persisting, they termed it as spondylosis and told me not only to wear a collar and belt but also to change my mattress and pillow. That's when I met my Reiki Angel in disguise, and with just 3-4 minutes of Reiki healing for 3 days, she facilitated the healing by getting my body back in balance, which relieved me from the persisting discomfort that had been making my life miserable for more than one and a half years! I haven't looked back since then. My daily self-healing is consistent, and I know that Reiki is there with me at all times, be it for emotional, mental, physical, or spiritual healing. As a silent guide, it has been leading me towards various holistic practices, which are a boon, as I'm blessed to be able to help others overcome challenging situations.

Over the past couple of years, I have been meeting people who, at times, have learned Reiki before me but are out of practice since they haven't been using it. It really saddens me to see their wonderful gift going to waste when that can heal so many around them. The natural instinct is to get them back to their wonderful Reiki practice and experience the divine natural healing energy. The experience of being able to help others restart their Reiki practice motivated me to conduct the 21-day workshops, which helped them kick-start their daily Reiki practice and heal others, too. The success of the 21-day workshops and the urging of my daughter are what motivated me to put that workshop material into book form, which is in your hands today. I sincerely hope that this book will inspire the lost Reiki channels to find their path back to healing and enriched life.

Meditation link for Days 2, 7, 8, 14, 16 & 18

How to Scan a QR Code:

1. Open your camera app.

2. Point your camera at the QR code.

3. Tap the notification that appears.

Alternative Method:

1. Download a QR code scanner app.

2. Open the app and scan the QR code.

Make sure the QR code is well-lit and fully visible in the camera frame.

Day 1

Let's start with

OM MANI PADME HUM, and that's for a reason.

This Buddhist mantra is related to invoking compassion, and you need it most for yourself as everything starts with you. It's your existence which makes things happen for you, and that's what brings about the various pleasant or unpleasant experiences. These experiences create memories, and the disturbing ones create blocks that are stored in the body as knots.

So, let's begin with the self.

OM: Dissolves Ego and Pride. It's composed of A, U and M symbolising the impure body, speech and mind, and also symbolises the pure body, speech and mind of a Buddha.

MANI: Meaning jewel, symbolises its capability of removing poverty (mental) or difficulties of cyclic existence and of peace.

PADME: Padme, meaning lotus, symbolises wisdom, just as the lotus grows in mud but does not carry its traits. Similarly, wisdom is capable of bringing you to a situation of non-contradiction.

HUM: Hum indicates indivisibility of method and wisdom.

Hum is the seed syllable of Akshobhya - the immovable, the unfluctuating, that which cannot be disturbed by anything.

Hence, this mantra means that if you practice a path of the union of method and wisdom, then you can transform your impure body, speech and mind to the pure body, speech and mind of a Buddha.

You already have the seed of purity within and you just need to awaken it!

Meditation:

Sit in a quiet place where you won't be disturbed.

If possible, sit in Padma (lotus) posture and hold Chin Mudra (tips of thumb and index finger touching lightly).

Close your eyes and take 3 deep breaths.

Chant OM MANI PADME HUM 108 times.

Notes

Notes

Day 2

Why did you choose to learn Reiki?

Did you learn to heal so that you could heal others?

Did you experience healing before you opted to learn?

Did you have a disease or discomfort that led you there?

Did you know someone who was healed with Reiki and thought of giving it a try?

Did you just go along because your friend or loved one was learning and learned it?

Whatever the reason might have been for your initiation to Reiki, trust me, your Reiki works both for you and the healee.

Reiki does not discriminate and flows the same for all who have gone through a physical attunement with a trained Master.

You don't choose Reiki, Reiki chooses you!

"To attune" means "to bring into harmony." So, when your Master initiated you, the Chakras were opened up, and certain blockages were removed. You started on a journey of becoming "whole" by allowing energy to flow freely through your palms and/or soles of your feet, thus becoming a healer.

The attunement process raises your vibrations to connect to the limitless source of Universal Energy, thus making you a channel for energy transfer.

If for some reason, which could even be fear of the unknown, you were unable to surrender completely to the attunement process and received it with any form of doubt, then let me take you through a receiving guided exercise..... accept this meditation "The Gift from the Masters" with complete surrender.

Follow this guided exercise (you can record and play):

Sit in a comfortable position...... remove your specs, clips, belt, if there,.... put your palms on your thighs, facing upwards,...... take a deep breath.... and centre yourself..... exhale relaxing your body completely..... visualise a beautiful golden box in your hands..... it's been sent to you by the Divine Masters.... slowly open and you see that there's a beautiful golden light coming out of the box.... allow it to cover you completely..... now visualise the violet at the Crown Chakra... it's expanding to fill your whole body... now visualise the colour Indigo at the Third Eye and allow it to expand completely.... visualise the colour Blue at the Throat Chakra.... allow it to expand and cover your whole body.... now bring your awareness to the Heart

Chakra and visualise the colour green... let it expand all around you.... now come to the Solar Plexus visualising the colour yellow and let it expand..... visualise yourself being covered with this yellow.... now come to the Hara visualising the colour orange.... allow it to expand surrounding you.... now come to the Root Chakra.... visualise the Red of the Root Chakra.... visualise it expanding and surrounding your whole circumference.... feel the energy in each and every tiny cell of your body.... sense the vibrations and sensations in your palms....now place the box on the side... put your palms together and thank the Masters for giving you this wonderful gift of healing.... thank Reiki for flowing through you and guiding you at all times.... take a deep breath and with a few blinks open your eyes... thank you Reiki.

Notes

Notes

Day 3

Self-healing is a very important component of Reiki.

Do you know why?

Read on.

Check yourself if you have been avoiding self-healings and finding excuses for not doing it. It could be cited as "lack of time", "too much work", "not feeling well", etc. etc.

Do you know that this is an indication that, consciously or unconsciously, you feel unworthy of LOVE and HEALING?

Have you ever thought along those lines?

INTROSPECT as to why you can't love yourself enough!

Maybe you're okay with giving healing to others but are reluctant when it comes to self - ask yourself why is it so that while you're willing to assist others in their journey to heal, you're avoiding your journey to wellness?

Routinely doing self-treatment will keep your channels clear of any toxins and negativity which accumulate throughout the day. If you require healing yourself, then the client will receive only partial energy since you are consuming on the way.

Benefits of Self-Healing:

- ➢ Pain Relief

- ➢ Better Sleep

- ➢ Boosts Energy

- ➢ Spiritual Growth

- ➢ Reduces Stress

- ➢ Pain Management

- ➢ Increases Creativity

- ➢ Helps in Conceiving

Affirmations for self, which can be used as required:

Always start with "Thank you, Reiki."

- ➢ I love myself just as I am

- ➢ I am open to receiving Goodness

- ➢ I am cool calm and relaxed at all times

- ➢ I live in complete harmony at all times

- ➢ I consume only healthy food and liquids

- ➢ I am happy with my spiritual progress

- ➢ I am open to receiving Divine Revelations

- ➢ My aches and pains have subsided at the earliest

- ➢ I have total clarity about the required actions

- ➢ I know what to do when to do and how to do

- ➢ My Reiki healing powers keep me energised

- ➢ I completely surrender, trusting the Reiki process

- ➢ My mind is still and I am one with my knowing self

Try these affirmations one at a time while healing yourself, and make a note of the changes you feel.

Some of them might resonate more than others, so you can use them accordingly.

Review after 7 days to see if you wish to make changes.

Shifts will happen so you can switch the affirmations accordingly.

Notes

Notes

Day 4

Reiki does not require any pre-treatment preparations, but having some of them can help set in a feeling of relaxation and become more receptive.

The Reiki principles teach us to live in the moment with a clear understanding that we actually don't get upset with what happens to us in life, but it's the reaction to those life circumstances which is the culprit.

Dr. USUI's precepts urge practitioners to live in the moment with awareness. You have to break away from the old patterns if you wish to let in the new.

They will also help you recognise that your anxieties and emotions are a hindrance to wellness.

As we rise spiritually, we tend to repress anger and feel we have managed it, but remember, extinguishing and repressing are different. You should not ignore your feelings of anger; instead, you should validate them. Express them but in a way which does not harm the harmony around you.

Living the 5 principles will help you achieve inner peace and harmony.

> ➢ Just for today, do not worry: Not worrying today takes care of your mental peace and automatically keeps you grounded.

> ➢ Just for today, do not be angry: Keeping your anger in control is more for your benefit than for others. In order to spew out anger, you first have to create it in yourself. Then only you can throw it out. If you don't have it within, it cannot be expressed.

> ➢ Just for today, I earn my living honestly: Whatever is being done by you should have your 100% in it. The commitment, the execution, everything should have your complete attention.

> ➢ Just for today, I honour my parents, teachers, and elders: Whether you have a good relationship with them or not, respect each and every elder because whatever you are today has some contribution from them, directly or indirectly.

> ➢ Just for today, I show gratitude to all living beings: Even the pen and pencil you hold deserve gratitude. In fact, all those things that we perceive as dead have some kind of energy in them, so we should have gratitude for each and every thing.

TIPS for remembering the 5 precepts which should be repeated at least once in the day -

➢ Write/ Print them and stick them on your phone, which you check multiple times a day.

➢ Make it your screensaver.

➢ You can stick tiny stickers around the house in places that you see many times a day, like a mirror, refrigerator, TV, etc.

➢ You can set alarm/s.

These can work as reminders and help you transform your life.

Notes

Notes

Day 5

Set an Intention but do not have any expectations, as they are 2 different things.

Intention empowers healing as it allows it to unfold naturally, whereas an expectation limits the healing process since holding an expectation amounts to human judgement and control.

With clients, setting an intention before the start of healing could be helpful in the process, as both you and the receiver will be working on the same thought and intention.

At those times when the recipient is not clear about the intention, then you, the practitioner, can suggest that the first treatment can be done with the focus of the recipient receiving clarity about the most significant needs. Thus, using "receiving clarity" as an intention could be powerful in reaching out directly to any illness or imbalance within the body.

As healers we do wish and hope that each client gets the best outcome, but we have to be clear about the fact that we're only facilitators.

While giving a healing the outcome is not in your hands. You're not the creator of anyone's healing journey. You're only a channel helping in the process so the client has to be fully participating in the flow of vital healing energy enabling them to reap the maximum benefits.

If you don't have expectations from the healing, then any outcome would be acceptable not only to you but also to the recipient.

The whole process should start without any expectations and end without any guilt. You should not be questioning or doubting your Reiki.

Your faith and belief in the healing powers of Reiki are what you will carry to the client.

Notes

Notes

Day 6

You might have just started using Reiki or might have been doing Reiki for years or months, treating the various Chakras.

Here, I'm sharing an exercise that will help you feel Reiki energy moving first towards your arms, and as it flows more and more, you will feel a pleasant tingling and flowing sensation wherever it reaches.

This will also help in releasing the blockages in your body and replace them with love, warmth and free flow of energy.

As this fills you with a sense of wholeness, you will feel and know that you are accepted.

This exercise will join the minor Chakras, both in your palms and soles and also the reflex points situated there. This will create a complete energetic circle.

A continuous flow will be created with the movement of energy between the Chakras, meridians and reflex zones within the body without any escape route. This enhanced power will release all kinds of blockages allowing you to experience the best flow possible.

During this exercise, you need to breathe through your stomach. Start with 2 minutes, and you can increase the duration gradually.

To Further Expand the Energy:

➤ You can chant OM and/or

➤ Hold a small Rose Quartz Crystal between your palms

To Do This Exercise:

➤ You can rest against a wall to keep yourself comfortable

➤ You can sit on the bed

➤ You can sit on the mat

➤ You can lie on your back

Whichever position you take, be sure that you're comfortable and keep your palms together and soles together at all times.

THIS EXERCISE, WITH THE COMBINED FLOW OF YOUR LIFE ENERGY, WILL EXPAND THE LIMITS OF YOUR PERCEPTION AND INCREASE POSSIBILITIES OF YOUR SELF EXPRESSION.

You will definitely enjoy this meditative exercise.

Second and Third-Degree Channels can reinforce and enhance this beautiful experience by incorporating the Reiki symbols.

Palms and Feet Meditative Picture

Photo courtesy: Ms. Rupa Iyengar

Notes

Notes

Day 7

The past few days have been a learning of position, practice and usage along with exercises and meditations which will enhance and help you reach another level of healing self and others.

Reiki works in 7-day cycles, and today, the 7th day of your journey, is the day to visit your internal shifts, which are being noticed by you and those around you.

I would like you to write down your Reiki experiences which have occurred in the passing days, whether good or not so good. These could be any kind of a change. Pen down your reflections regarding your physical, mental, emotional, spiritual and social shifts.

Also, write down what your most commonly used reason is for forgetting yourself or putting yourself behind others.

Once you have written it down, read and re-read your progress, and notice the shifts that have already occurred or are required as you go further.

Practice the Heart Connection meditation

Lie down and make yourself comfortable....let your body relax....take a deep breath.... and e-x-h-a-l-e... shift your focus to your breath.... and as you inhale...and exhale.... allow your body to get more and more relaxed with each breath..... now take a long deep breath and slowly put your right hand on your heart.... slowly put your left hand on the Hara which is below the navel... imagine that you're being filled to the brim with love.... there is immense love both outside and inside you....gradually take your attention to the heart...feel it being filled with the golden bright light of love... you're slowly getting more and more relaxed... now imagine this golden light centring like a golden ball in your heart....from your heart this energy is slowly expanding to touch every part of your body... start with your head...let the love energy touch it.... mentally express love to every part.... your hair... brain... forehead.... eyes... eyebrows... nose... cheeks... lips... teeth... mouth.... ears... and chin....come down to your neck...the food pipe... the wind pipe... cover them all with love...come to your shoulders and upper back... send love energy to the lungs and to the heart itself which is the centre of all love....take it to each of the hands...and to your stomach...pancreas...and liver...spread the love to your lower abdomen...take it to your genitals and each leg...now your entire body is covered in love....it is like being in the lap of your mother...never before have you experienced such deep intense love...now turn your attention to the heart....the heart has always been there for you...beating ceaselessly... pumping blood and providing you with energy and vitality... from the first breath to your last...the heart is there with you throughout...unlike what you might have believed the heart is emotional and thereby irrational...however... it is holistic.... being connected to the cosmic computer...it can sense what most of our senses and rational thoughts miss...thank this heart for serving you tirelessly all the while...express your gratitude to this wonderful organ...which many believe is the seed of the mind...the responses of the heart are never in words...they are in feelings... a feeling of comfort is a positive response... it's comfort is never negative... it's more the way your heart makes you feel... learning to recognise this is very important...for going beyond this process...the first question to ask your heart is whether it is willing to talk to you...wait a little...if you feel the response is that of discomfort repeat the request a few times...ask your heart again...just give it time....your heart loves you and will agree.....however if you're not comfortable with it...the heart will give you a negative response... if that is the case do not force the heart....let go...express gratitude...and you can end the process here...you could lie for sometime and relax....and if your heart wishes to talk to you ask your heart if you really love yourself....so many of us have never taken time to actually love ourselves...maybe it is the conditioning that we received in our childhood... it even might have been something to do with your values...but you need to realise that loving yourself is of utmost importance.... listen to the response...as it will give you some realisation about yourself...now ask whether you take enough care of yourself... you might be ignoring yourself for priorities related to others... or maybe you just don't care enough....whatever it might be.... it doesn't make sense to ignore yourself... your body is the temple of God and you need to treat it with respect...ask your heart if you're physically and mentally fit...are you really living at the level where you want to be... or maybe you deserve more....now ask...whether you take care of yourself....and about your likes and dislikes...maybe you're failing to pay attention to the seemingly unimportant things....give your heart sometime... let it respond.... the heart never lies.... now thank your heart for helping you through this process...and say I love you.... slowly...make yourself comfortable for coming out from this process..... if you wish you can lie down for some time and finish the process whenever you feel comfortable.

Notes

Notes

Day 8

Your physical body is made up of trillions of cells and your energy field penetrates to those cells affecting them as per experiences.

All your experiences, whether positive or negative, are carried as expressions of your consciousness and many negative experiences, which "don't seem too bad" at the mental level, might have created many imbalances within your energy field.

Today, I'm sharing a Cells Healing Meditation.

Reiki will flow where it's desired; hence, your acceptance and openness to receiving this healing energy will dictate the level of energy you receive.

You have your own unique response to Reiki healing energy, and that will decide your cell regeneration.

In order for Reiki to work effectively, please be open to receiving the healing energy.

This session will assist you in stimulating your regeneration process.

Drink some water…just relax and allow the healing to happen.

Follow the Process:

Sit comfortably with your eyes closed....place your hands wherever comfortable...see yourself approaching a beautiful waterfall...that cascades gently to a shallow placid lake as you get closer to this waterfall...you're able to see that the waterfall is made of drops of beautiful healing blue or whatever colour you choose as your healing colour....the water is the same colour...you wade to the soft pool of water... untill you're directly under this gentle waterfall... feel this soft and cool healing water.... feel each and every drop as it begins to penetrate through the top of your head...flowing through...and into the top of your head...guide it down...down... down....until it reaches your heart... feel this cool healing blue water as it enters your blood stream..pumps through each cell in your body...cleansing...calming...coolling...healing every cell... every nerve...and every fibre of your body... feel it as it is flowing through you now...through your shoulders...down your arms to your fingertips...back up your elbows.... back to your chest...to your heart...this cool blue healing light and water is now flowing down through your stomach... cooling and healing all of the organs in your middle body...your intestines...down...down.. through your hips... your thighs... your knees... the calves...your ankles...your toes...now you see this blue light penetrating each and every cell of your body...the tiniest of cells...f-e-e-l it as it is clearing and refreshing every cell...healing every cell... making it well...healthy...and whole... well...healthy... and whole...complete...you are now one with this placid lake... as placid...calm...and peaceful as the lake...allow the healing to flow through you...allow yourself to be a calm...

cool...drop in the lake.... you're one with the lake... you're well...healthy...whole... and...complete... you're one with the lake...flowing down...cleansing every cell...see every cell as new...healthy...well...and whole...each and every time that you follow this meditation..it will reinforce the message... healthy...well...whole...and complete... and it is so because you order your cells to be healthy...well... and whole...say to yourself..if there are any cells that exist in my body that are not all complete...healthy... and...whole....I instruct my body to wash them out with this blue healing water...flush them out...through my system...so that they can be r-e-l-e-a-s-e-d and disposed of....transmuted and changed to healthy..well and whole cells exist in this body... this temple of mine that I love and respect...I am a vessel for healthy cells...cells that respect my body...and make it well...and free of disease...I live in harmony with the universe....all of my cells respond to my voice...as I intend for them...all...each and every one of them to be healthy.... well...complete...and whole....ten times well...my cells are healthy...well...whole and complete..and it is so because I ordain it... I am a child of the universe...I deserve to be healthy...my cells are healthy...I am healthy. Every day, in every way, I manifest great health and happiness in my life. I am happy... I am whole. Each and every time I see or sense the colour blue, I am healed, and it is so. Thank you Reiki, for making it so.

Notes

Notes

Day 9

By now, I hope you're healing others, at least one other person.

I always say, "The more you give, the more you receive."

Every time you give a healing to someone, you yourself are going through one.

If you haven't started … what is keeping you from doing it?

You can start with a family member.

Acute Problems, lying dormant, which have come up to the surface and are making themselves known should also be checked out by a doctor while you can start giving healing for a correct diagnosis.

Since Reiki sends a lot of powerful Universal Energy to the area, you or the healee might feel some irritation or discomfort, which is natural. Here, it is to be understood that this usually is a positive sign that energy is being drawn so the healing will be faster.

Notes

Day 10

In today's fast-paced, high-tech world, people are looking for a simple method to deal with stress, relaxation, and healing.

Touch has always been a very important human need, and Reiki physical healing provides that loving kindness and acceptance.

Having worked with Reiki, you're very much aware that Reiki works in harmony with all other healing practices, such as natural, homoeopathy, chiropractic, nutritional, acupuncture, reflexology, and all others.

Reiki works safely with Western medicine and prescription drugs, surgery and medical procedures.

Researchers have been studying the efficacy of Reiki, and there are several studies that validate Reik's healing properties.

With the help of Krilian sensing, one can see an individual's aura increase after a Reiki treatment. The before and after pictures clearly demonstrate the healing effect.

The scientific-minded people wish to know if Reiki actually works or if it's just a placebo effect.

One of the studies (Autonomous Neuron-System-Change During Reiki Treatment) did an experiment where groups were divided into those who received Reiki Healing from Reiki channels and the other group from those who were not attuned to Reiki (placebo). Vital statistics were recorded, including heart rate, blood pressure, temperature and respiration.

The study revealed a significant reduction in diastolic blood pressure and heart rate in those who received actual Reiki healing, which didn't appear in the placebo group.

There was another study which recorded the effect of Reiki on the White Blood cell count. Blood was drawn before the treatment, immediately after treatment and 4 hours after treatment. The conclusion was that Reiki enhanced the immune system by increasing the number of white cells in those who received Reiki healing.

It's always beneficial to heal others as it strengthens your own practice and faith when the clients get healed. Also, every time that you give a healing, you go through one, too.

2nd Degree and above should apply the symbols at all points.

If you're on any medication, then hold the pills in your palms and Reiki them before consuming. This will not only increase the efficacy but also take care of side and after effects.

Notes

Notes

Day 11

Achieving Goals with Reiki

Whether you realise it or not, the subtle vibrations which surround things can have the greatest impact on the decisions you make.

If you focus on improving the vibrations of whatever you want, the results can be impressive.

What is the best way to do this?

By sending Reiki to your project, task or goal.

If you're looking to achieve your goal, then adding Reiki to the process will raise the quality and make the achievement much smoother and easier.

Remember: At all times, Reiki works for the highest good of all concerned.

Your goal should be in harmony with the consciousness of Reiki; otherwise, Reiki will not work.

With Reiki, you cannot harm or wish harm for others, and you cannot control them against their will.

Supposing you have done your best in choosing your goal, but there's still something out of balance, Reiki will help you understand what changes are required so that they align with the well-being of all concerned.

In order to receive guidance and fruitful results, do the following exercise:

1. Write your goal on a card or paper.

2. Place it in one hand

➢ Level 1 channels cover with the other hand and keep thanking Reiki for the right guidance and fulfilment.

➢ Level 2 and above, draw the power symbol over it while sending light for a few seconds, then cover it.

3. While placed between your palms, give Reiki from 3-10mins.

4. You will know what needs to be done, so take action accordingly.

5. Give Reiki to your card/paper every day. The best would be to give Reiki in the morning soon after awakening and at night before sleeping.

6. You can carry the card with you and give Reiki whenever you get a few spare moments.

Reiki will start flowing to those areas of your mind which are connected to the goal.

Blocks and restrictions will disappear, and if any facet of your personality resists them, that area will be healed.

Reiki will help you to be at the right place at the right time and connect with the right people who matter.

There's a great possibility of you getting more than what you had imagined as you follow the inner guidance inspired by Reiki.

Word of caution: just because you have set a goal for yourself doesn't mean that it's the best for you. Trust Reiki since it knows better than you. If the results aren't as per your expectations, then be sure that they aren't the best for you. We see the short term, but Universal Energy sees the long term.

2nd level and above (Distant Healing)- The same goes for your clients. They might tell you to do Reiki for a certain thing, which might give a different result, so it's entirely your conviction which will help you tackle that.

Have faith, trust it, and get awesome results!

It depends on you entirely!

Notes

Notes

Day 12

Blessing and Clearing Rooms

One of the reasons for people getting sick or work and life getting stuck is because the flow of their life energy is blocked in some areas.

You can get this moving by sending Reiki energy to that area.

You could be using your room for healing, sleeping, work, meetings, entertainment or anything else, but if you're in that room even for a fraction of the day, then you're absorbing the energies present in that room.

Remember, it's easier to pass and absorb negative energies than the positive ones.

You would benefit greatly by clearing the following spaces -

➢ A space that has stagnant energy

➢ A hotel room that was previously occupied by unknown people

> A room that has witnessed people releasing their negative energies

> A room that does not give good vibes or makes you feel uncomfortable.

> Your own room where you might have had a couple of unpleasant thoughts or interactions.

Technique

Level 1:

1. Light a candle or lamp and sit in the centre of the room.

2. Take 3 deep breaths to balance your energies.

3. Clap your hands 3 times, saying "Thank you, Reiki," then place your hands on your thighs, palms facing downwards, and give yourself Reiki for a few minutes.

4. Now visualise the Divine White Reiki Light filling up the room completely… see it all around on each and every wall.

5. As you see the room fill up with energy 3 times say, "I bless this room with Reiki."

6. Be with the energy for some time and then disconnect while thanking Reiki.

Level 2 and Above:

1. Light a candle or lamp.

2. Sit in the centre of the room, draw the Power Symbol in your palms, and clap your hands 3 times, saying the name of the sacred symbol to yourself.

3. Place your hands on your thighs, palms facing downwards, and give yourself Reiki for a few minutes.

4. Now look at the wall in front of you, and, with uplifted hands, draw the Power Symbol with Radiant Reiki Light, saying the name thrice. Say, "I bless this room with Reiki." Repeat this with the other walls, floor, and ceiling.

5. End the session by thanking Reiki as you visualise the room filled with Divine Reiki Light.

You can do this for all the rooms and your kitchen too.

Notes

Notes

Day 13

Reiki for Protection

If you feel negative energy around you, the first thing to do is to send Reiki to the negative energy. This way, it can be neutralised and healed.

After that, look within and see which parts of you have manifested this experience and heal them.

After that, strengthen your energy field, fill the cracks in your aura, which allow leaks, and sense the Chakras, which require healing.

A strengthened aura and balanced Chakras act as protective barriers. You have allowed some interference to adversely affect you, so you need to heal those areas.

Do this exercise for Strengthening your Aura.

Level 1:

1. Sit on a chair and bring your palms together. Stay for a couple of minutes to get the energy activated, then thank Reiki and place your hands on your thighs. Give Reiki to yourself for a couple of minutes.

2. Now, Visualise your God, Deity or any higher being you believe in and send Reiki.

3. Request the enlightened being to help you strengthen your Aura and help you heal the reason why you attracted the negativity.

4. Now Visualise your Aura and Chakras being perfect and healthy,

Repeat 3 times: "My Aura is becoming Stronger and Stronger and Stronger."

5. If you still feel gaps, you can stay with them longer.

6. If you feel that a specific area is holding the negative block, send Reiki directly to that area.

7. Feel yourself radiating with Divine Reiki energy and say "I seal this session with Reiki Light."

8. My Aura has been strengthened, and I am fully protected hold this thought, take a deep breath and open your eyes slowly.

Level 2 and Above:

1. Sit on a chair, draw the Power Symbol on your palms, thank Reiki and stay for a couple of minutes. Then, place your hands on your thighs and give Reiki to yourself for a couple of minutes.

2. Draw the Distance Symbol in front of you and start sending Reiki to an enlightened being, your God, Deity or anyone else whom you believe.

3. Request the higher being to help you heal the root cause of why you attracted the negative energy.

4. Draw the Power Symbol in front of you and repeat 3 times, "My aura is becoming Stronger and Stronger and Stronger."

If you still feel gaps, you can repeat.

5. If you feel that a specific area is holding the negative block, focus on that area, draw the Power Symbol and send Reiki energy to that area. Cover yourself with the Power Symbol on all sides.

6. Your Aura has been strengthened with Divine energy and you are protected with Divine Reiki Light.

7. "I am feeling whole and complete" hold this thought, take a deep breath and open your eyes slowly.

Notes

Notes

Day 14

Surrender and Gratitude

Gratitude is a very important component of Reiki practice.

One of the 5 precepts of Reiki is "Show gratitude to all living beings."

A reminder here that in Reiki even a pen, pencil, book, table, etc is considered as living since it's made up of tiny cells and molecules and has contributed to our life directly or indirectly.

Practice the following Reiki meditation with complete acceptance and surrender.

This meditation will increase your connection to the Source and make it stronger.

Most likely, you will have interesting experiences while in meditation and throughout the day.

Receive whatever comes your way with deep gratitude and allow yourself to be guided to the processes that will enhance your life.

Meditation

Sit comfortably…..and allow your body to r-e-l-a-x …..draw the Reiki symbols on your hands …if you don't have Reiki symbols this process will still work…place your hands on your thighs and allow the Reiki energy to begin flowing…. feel it spreading within you….down to your feet …and flowing up to your head…allow yourself to merge with the feelings of warmth…peace …or any other feelings coming from the Reiki energy..accept whats coming your way ….. now say "I am grateful for the healing power of Reiki ….and I surrender completely with loving care and to the Source from which it comes…I am grateful for the healing power of Reiki and surrender completely to its loving care and to the Source from which it comes …I am grateful for the healing power of Reiki and surrender completely…..to its loving care and to the Source from which it comes…..now….with your inner eye…imagine looking up through the top of your head and look for the Source of Reiki ….as you continue …imagine….moving closer and closer to the Source of Reiki….repeat …I am grateful for the healing power of Reiki ….and I surrender completely to its loving care …and to the Source from which it comes …I am grateful for the healing powers of Reiki and surrender completely to its loving care and the Source from which it comes … I am grateful for the healing power of Reiki …and surrender completely…. to its loving care…. and the Source from which it comes…. bring your palms together …place them at the heart …. bow down in surrender and gratitude…thank Reiki…come up…. take a d-e-e-p breath exhaling through the mouth…...and slowly open your eyes….

Notes

Notes

Day 15

Spiritual Growth and Reiki

Our purpose in life is to connect to the Divine Source from which we originated.

If that is the uppermost thought in your mind, then Reiki, being the intelligent energy that it is, will guide you towards that path according to your openness and willingness.

When connection with the Source diminishes, it keeps us from reaching our full potential.

By using Reiki for self and for others, you are opening up the channels of reconnecting with the Divine Source, and you can even use Reiki to connect directly to that source.

Your life's conditioning and experiences have led you to make certain decisions, which have created varied habits that limit the help you can receive from the Divine Source.

Reiki respects your Free Will, so if you wish to enhance your growth, then you not only have to ask for help from the Source, but you also have to be willing and open to making the changes which come up to allow the old patterns to break away and the new ones to emerge.

Your spiritual life will start giving you everyday experiences with the new beginnings. Sometimes they might not seem what you were seeking but have faith that it is that which is required for your growth.

As you start building up your spiritual journey, the new patterns which emerge will provide you with a chance to learn to be less in control and more of giving up, of letting go, while trusting the flow of life.

As this happens be open to trying out the new ways of feeling, being and doing and sticking to them as they will help you in releasing your stress and help you to grow in a positive manner.

Ask Reiki to help you raise your spiritual vibrations. Also, while self-healing, allow Reiki to guide you toward your spiritual purpose.

As you raise your vibrational energy, you might be challenged to learn new things so that you can overcome your old unconscious fears, personal blocks, and negative patterns, leading you to heal them. At these times, remember that Reiki will help you in this journey of healing and growing.

When your purpose is driven by love for the Source of Reiki, yourself, and others, you will see that other people will sense this and be more supportive in helping you achieve your spiritual purpose.

Once you start getting into greater alignment with the Source, things will start happening in joyful and mysterious ways. If you ever face times when the change appears difficult, remind yourself that since this is a part of the growth experience, this change has come as a reminder to re-centre yourself in love because there's something which requires healing (doing the Heart Meditation will help).

Wishing you a wonderful spiritual journey!

Notes

Notes

Day 16

Reiki White Light Meditation

You can use this Reiki meditation for:

- times when you feel low in energy

- when you just "don't feel good" and are unable to pinpoint the reason

- when you have an unpleasant interaction with someone

- for manifesting your intentions

- if you're feeling anxious

- in a state of depression

- if you're feeling restlessness

Preparation

1. Choose to sit in a place where you won't be disturbed.

2. Remove belt, wallet, hairclips, phone and watch. You don't need to remove jewellery.

3. Drink some water.

4. It is very important to keep your eyes closed throughout the session. The entire effect will be lost the moment you open your eyes in between. Open them only when instructed to do so.

5. If you're seeking fulfilment of some intention, keep it uppermost in your mind before you begin.

Follow the meditation:

Sit comfortably....leaving your body loose...take a deep breath...and e-x-h-a-l-e.....close your eyes and start breathing deeply...as you inhale...the stomach rises up and as you exhale it sinks in...i-n-h-a-l-e.....and e-x-h-a-l-e......inhale....and...exhale.... relaxing the whole body... relax...relax...now visualise a huge ball of brilliant white light over your Crown Chakra...this is a huge ball...covering the whole area above your head...shining brightly....this radiant light is ready to enter your body....now visualise and feel the brilliant light entering your body through the Crown Chakra...the energy of the white light... is filling up your head....your neck...your shoulders...your arms...and your hands...going down to the Heart Chakra...take a deep breath... this brilliant white light is filling up your abdomen... and is cascading down towards your feet....filling up your legs as it is going down... the whole body is filled with this divine bright light....which is so free flowing....you can feel the energy filling you up....now bring your attention to the Heart Chakra....and exactly the way Reiki flows through it.... this beautiful divine light is spreading out from you...and you can feel that it has filled up the whole room...you can see the room covered with this divine white light...let it expand further over your entire house... now allow it to expand further covering all the houses in your neighbourhood.... keep expanding...keep expanding this brilliant white light.... which started emanating from you...your heart....and let it go further....further and further.... covering the entire city..... it's expanding further to cover your country... visualise and see it expanding to the whole earth....and all its beings.... allow this brilliant white light to expand further... to cover the whole universe...the planets...stars.. milky way... and further to the galaxies... believe in yourself and keep expanding it....your source is limitless... now visualise your intention exactly as you want it...as this is what will manifest...add all the details to it...even the minutest....now cover this with the divine white light...praying for the highest good of all concerned...bring your focus back to your heart.... take a deep breath.... and exhale.... say Thank you Reiki for fulfilling my intention.... only when you feel comfortable to do so....slowly open your eyes...you can take your time.... Thank you Reiki....

Notes

Notes

Day 17

" …. All strength, all healing of every nature is the changing of vibrations from within - the attuning of the Divine within the living tissue of a body to Creative Energies. This alone is healing."

"For the Mind is the Builder - as a man thinketh so is he - so does that mind, that body, that soul, expand to meet the needs of same."

- Edgar Cayce

Today, we have more cancer, heart disease, diabetes, high blood pressure, high cholesterol, mental illnesses and, even birth defects.

You are blessed that you already have the tool of Reiki with you, which works in all 4 areas, namely - mental, physical, emotional, and spiritual.

The ability required is to use it to treat the body and mind in a nurturing and life-enhancing manner.

Stress creates havoc not only in the body but also in all its layers and Reiki is that subtle energy which can not only control stress but also remove it altogether, depending on your faith and commitment.

You need to learn to be in the present moment rather than the past or future. If that's too tall a task to handle, seek help from the Reiki precepts…. "Just for Today….."

Tip: Place tiny stickers around the house where your gaze travels frequently, or keep it as your screen saver, serving as a constant reminder of the 5 precepts. That will help you keep your mind in balance.

Again, it makes sense only if feelings are attached to it otherwise it will not fetch the desired result.

You can use one of the meditations, depending on your availability, to reach a state of calmness.

Doing a healing when you go to sleep will reinforce your beliefs, whatever you have chosen to believe in.

Know that your body, mind, spirit, and emotions will respond to your suggestions… whatever the mind conceives and believes, it will achieve ….. The choice is always yours … it is you who chooses to heal or not!

Look within for your answer of whether you're happy or not! If not, then your body, mind and/or spirit is seeking attention for balance. Give more Reiki to yourself and bring your body in balance.

Notes

Notes

Day 18

Having practised Reiki, at least whenever required, and with feedback from your clients, you know that it works!

Also, you are aware of how stress works on your physical body. Life keeps bringing newer challenges, which at times feel like a burden and stress you out, so here is a Reiki healing which will truly lighten you by the end of it.

If it doesn't, then you need to be introspective and honest as to what needs to be accepted.

Allow yourself to be open to receiving whatever comes up for you.

Close your eyes..... Take a deep breath in and exhale... another breath in and as you exhale release all the tension from your body...breathe in....and exhale.... put your palms together....and Thank Reiki...for healing you...internally and externally....place your palms on the Third Eye and visualise the colour indigo there....place your palms on the Crown Chakra...visualising the colour violet....take your hands to the back Third Eye and visualise the colour indigo once again.... place your palms on the Throat Chakra...

covering the throat and thorax...visualise the colour blue..... place your palms on the Heart Chakra centre with fingertips touching and visualise the colour green.....healing your heart completely... now place your palms on the Solar Plexus.... visualising the colour yellow..... and allow it to heal you.... now take your hands to the Hara.....visualising the colour orange.... feeling it spreading through.... now place your palms on the Root Chakra...visualising the colour Red.... after sufficient healing bring your palms together in folded position and place them in the centre of your chest..... feel and tune in to the vibrations in your body.... connect to all the pulsations.... Thank Reiki for giving you the abundance of health..wealth...and happiness.....Thank you Reiki....with a few blinks open your eyes....

Notes

Notes

Day 19

Quick Treatment

There can be situations where you wish to give Reiki but there simply isn't enough time or maybe it's an elderly or ailing person who might not be able to take a full body healing.

In such cases, you can resort to a quick form of healing that covers all the important positions.

Word of caution here that this does not constitute a complete full body healing and is to be used only if it's absolutely necessary.

However much time you have at that moment, make use of it and start the Quick Treatment in a calm manner. Never give the impression of being in a hurry. As I always say, Some Reiki is better than None.

At a slow pace, move through the following steps for the Quick Treatment-

1. Make the client sit or stand in their comfort zone, and you should stand on their side, having easy access.

2. Tell the client to thank Reiki and be receptive.

3. Say the Attitude of Gratitude

4. Place one hand on the front Third Eye and the other on the back Third Eye

5. Place one hand on the front Throat Chakra and the other on the back Throat Chakra.

6. Place one hand on the front Heart and the other on the back Heart

7. Place one hand on the front solar plexus and the other on the back solar plexus.

8. Place one hand on the front Hara and the other on the back Hara.

9. Sandwich the Left Knee and then the Right Knee.

10. Sweep the Energy from the Knees to the Crown.

11. Say the Attitude of Gratitude and cross your fingers or wash your hands.

12. Tell the client to Thank Reiki.

Notes

Notes

Day 20

It has been well established that people who are prone to negative feelings like sadness, anxiety, pessimism, anger, jealousy and stress are definitely more prone to develop disease.

The brain and the immune system work in sync, so a better state of mind always creates better health.

Both Reiki and meditation work together to heal the main "cause" of disease by working on the "psyche" of the human mind as spirit, as in the higher consciousness.

When Reiki starts to work on the higher consciousness (spiritual body), it tends to bring calmness to the Nervous System by opening up to the Higher Energies and integrating them as required for the healing flow of Reiki energy.

If you avoid taking full responsibility for your own physical maintenance, for the well-being and the loving nurturing care of your body then disease is what follows because of lack of caring.

Your conscious choice for change of reaction towards the people or environment will create a ripple effect through your system and will reach your Master Control Centre which is your brain.

You can always say, "Just for today, I choose to be Healthy and Happy."

This conscious choice will allow your body to heal itself, the tissues, the motor functions, your digestion and your responses.

Balance your energies since poor Ki circulation leads to impaired thoughts, actions, insomnia, mental disturbances, etc.

Remember that in Reiki, the best defence against disease of any kind is the achievement of and maintenance of a sense of well-being.

With clients, remember to share your beliefs about self-healing and motivating them to treasure and protect themselves with Reiki.

Teach them the importance of maintaining a healthy mind, body and spirit by allowing Reiki to flow through and helping others on all levels to experience the integration of love and inter connectedness.

Maybe, it would be the first time that they might be experiencing Unconditional Love and that would be the first step towards true healing of self.

Notes

Notes

Day 21

Reiki Tips and Tools:

➢ It is advisable to avoid negative thoughts and people. Still, if you're put in a situation where you can't avoid it, and you're forced into an argument or to listen to negativity, then while in the situation, interlock your fingers and place them on the Solar Plexus, mentally affirming "Thank you, Reiki I am in charge of myself I am cool and calm."

➢ After finishing the Attitude of Gratitude, say, "Thank you, Reiki. All healings channelled through me are a Reiki Success."

➢ If you are on medication, then give Reiki to them before consuming.

➢ Energise your food and water by placing your hands and palms facing down over the food and water.

➢ If you're going to a place where it's difficult to find parking then before you leave start affirming "Thank you Reiki for giving me a parking at....."

➢ Before you leave home, cover yourself with the Reiki Divine light and that will protect you from negative attacks.

➢ If an ailment is not getting diagnosed, then affirm, "Thank you, Reiki, for the correct diagnosis."

➢ If you're getting worried about your loved one then visualise him/her and give the Reiki protection by putting them in the Reiki White Light bubble.

➢ For overall growth and abundance, affirm, "Thank you, Reiki, for the abundance of health, wealth and happiness in my life."

➢ Children below 12 years would require only one minute at each Chakra.

➢ If you're running late for an appointment, use Reiki and see how it works.

➢ Channels 2nd level and above can carry the small Antahkarna for well-being and protection.

I wish you a wonderful Reiki journey ahead as the healing continues….

I'm grateful to you for giving me the opportunity to be your guide for 21 days of Reiki.

Thank you.

Notes

Notes

13 Reiki Positions

We treat the 7 major Chakras both front and back.

Altogether, we treat 13 points since the Crown Chakra is only treated once.

1.   Third Eye

2.   Crown

3.   Back Third Eye

4.   Throat and Thorax

5.   Heart

6.   Solar Plexus

7.   Hara

8.   Root

9.   Back Throat

10. Back Heart

11. Back Solar Plexus

12. Back Hara

13. Back Root

Basic Principles of Reiki Healing

1. Reiki can never do any harm.

2. Reiki is always given on asking.

3. Reiki is also given to plants and animals.

4. The healer shouldn't attach to the result.

5. Healer's energies are never depleted.

6. Reiki flow depends on the demand of the body.

7. Reiki treatment is equally effective for self and others.

8. Healing is not done by the healer. The healer is only a medium.

9. Reiki channels can feel warmth, heat, cold, circles, pull, etc., under the palm while healing.

10. Reiki also travels to other areas apart from where the hands are placed.

11. Reiki is an intelligent energy and flows to wherever it's required.

12. Some Reiki is better than no Reiki.

13. Reiki can be given to another even if self-healing hasn't been done.

www.ingramcontent.com/pod-product-compliance
Lightning Source LLC
Chambersburg PA
CBHW031304130726
47988CB00007B/2718